PRAISE
UMBILICAL

"Hasan Namir's new collection expands on his poetic oeuvre, this time turning his lens to his own growing family. This book brings to light the connections that bind us, and the complex ways traditions of domesticity impact how we view our own families, and others. In *Umbilical Cord*, poems are about the complicated, intimate and expansive ways of growing a family, and the cords necessary, to connect and to cut, that build a life."
　　　　　—Dina Del Bucchia, author of *Don't Tell Me What to Do*

"What does it mean to be a good father *and* a good son? Hasan Namir's *Umbilical Cord* is an intimate exploration of a new family forming and transforming in and against the tug and pull of generational, cultural and societal expectations. Loss and acceptance coexist on every page, the urgency in the text often held in the quiet of the whitespace. Part memoir, part love letter, *Umbilical Cord* threads together an imperfect life with a forgiving stitch—each poem with an *I* on joy."
　　　　　—Chantal Gibson, author *How She Read*

"The poems in *Umbilical Cord* are a deeply personal, and often heartbreaking, account of two men in love who find a way to have the child they so badly want. This book brings to light the transformative experience of creating a family despite bigotry, and adversity and the promises of unconditional love every parent makes. When Hasan Namir tells his son, 'I could scream and let the whole world know/You are our euphoria,' we swallow these words as witnesses."
　　　　　—Adrienne Gruber, author of *Q & A*

Umbilical Cord

Hasan Namir

Umbilical Cord

Hasan Namir

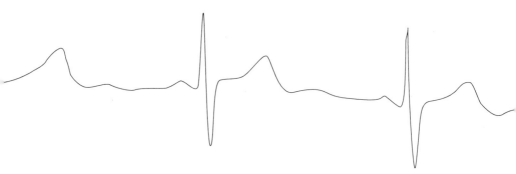

Book*hug Press
Toronto 2021

Library and Archives Canada Cataloguing in Publication

Title: Umbilical cord / Hasan Namir.

Names: Namir, Hasan, 1987– author.

Description: Poems.

Identifiers: Canadiana (print) 20210256192 | Canadiana (ebook) 20210256230

ISBN 9781771667180 (softcover)

ISBN 9781771667197 (EPUB)

ISBN 9781771667203 (PDF)

Classification: LCC PS8627.A536 U53 2021 | DDC C811/.6—dc23

PRINTED IN CANADA

The production of this book was made possible through the generous assistance of the Canada Council for the Arts and the Ontario Arts Council. Book*hug Press also acknowledges the support of the Government of Canada through the Canada Book Fund and the Government of Ontario through the Ontario Book Publishing Tax Credit and the Ontario Book Fund.

Book*hug Press acknowledges that the land on which we operate is the traditional territory of many nations, including the Mississaugas of the Credit, the Anishnabeg, the Chippewa, the Haudenosaunee and the Wendat peoples. We recognize the enduring presence of many diverse First Nations, Inuit and Métis peoples and are grateful for the opportunity to meet, work, and learn on this territory.

Book*hug Press

This book is dedicated
to all the dads, moms, and parents
and their unique journeys

Contents

Dear Child
Once upon a time
Your baba fell in love with your dad
We got married and dreamt of having a baby
A roller coaster of emotions and feelings
We were always hopeful

It Takes Two

April 9, 2011:
The day we met
I saw my whole life through
Told you this a hundred times

Muscles popping
Grey vest
Twinkling eyes
Facial hair
Smiling tenderly

Don't call it love at first sight
Don't say you saw us too
Don't know how and why
Don't imagine us
Family

Your eyes to mine
That was it
You stepped back
I pulled forward

You and I
See-saw

Turkey Baster Method

A hundred dollars on Amazon

One quick phone call

An unplanned flight

One weekend

A quiet song

Ejaculate

Dear Child
I could feel your heart beating into mine
You were eager to meet your parents
You arrived sooner than expected
You were our miracle
Our life is forever yours

You and I

You and I eloping
Our legs
                dancing

Our breaths intertwining
You choke me
                fucking

You and I dividing
Our lips
                kissing

Our skin bulging
You come inside
                lovemaking

You and I multiplying
                baby-making

Was It the Time?

Was it the time...?

When you bent me over
Whispered you loved me

Or was it...?

When you were on top of me
We fucked for countless hours

Or was it...?

When I ejaculated in the bottle
The clinic air antiseptic

Or was it...?
When you sucked the cake
Off my cock, you said it was yummy

Or was it...?
When we were being romantic
Somewhat flirty you swooned

Or was it...?
That time
We spoke baby language

Dear Child
Can you hear my whispers?
I don't know what I did to deserve you
I love you more than anything
I'm learning to be patient
I am still waiting for you

Tarn Is Love

Your eyes lured me into years of us
I couldn't breathe, overwhelmed and terrified
I knew you as a black-and-white Facebook photo
Your voice transported me to a home so familiar

When I looked through your eyes, I saw us
Embarking on our journeys of tomorrow
A foreseeable future, a baby in a basket
It was a boy, but that didn't matter

I knew I wanted to marry you; how could I not rush?
How could I wait? I was confident in my feelings
Though I had doubts from you, I wanted you so bad
Could I marry you after one week of knowing you?

Your heart opens in your eyes, you take me to places
I never knew existed, or was my heart fooling me?
I knocked at your door and hoped you would respond
You smiled sideways, sensing those intimate moments

Engagement Photos

I'm a kangaroo mother
Holding you against my chest
Skin-to-skin magic
Skin to skin to help you grow

My struggle began

Engagement photos

Once upon a time
your father and I fell in love
It took six months for your dad
To say he wanted to be with me forever

In Canada, two men can marry each other
That's not possible in other countries
Your daddy and I are very lucky
We found love in a hopeless place

Our engagement song, a gathering of sixty
Friends and family who accepted our love
March 9, 2012:
Pink and purple were our colours

After your daddy and I got engaged
We posted our photos to celebrate our love
Our photos outed us
Our families found us out

Your grandfather disowned me

Dear Child
As I'm writing this to you
I hear your cries
I run for you
You stop crying
Your face mirrors mine

Two Men Can't Have Babies

Two men can't reproduce
"The baby is gonna grow up confused."
Shame on us

Sodomy is a sin
"Everyone says your baby's beautiful,
He's ass-ugly."

Gays can adopt if they want
"What about surrogacy?"
You can't afford it
"Shame."

Paying a surrogate is illegal in Canada
"Who is gonna wanna carry your baby?"
We'll keep dreaming instead

The Surrogates

Sperm + egg = baby
Two men physically can't have babies
We don't deny the biological factors

"You could adopt, you know."
An endless process
One document after another
Costs even higher
We wanted our own

"If you ever want a child, I'm here for you."

Four years washed over
Who was going to carry our child?

We asked friend A, B, C, D, E, F, G, H, I, J
We understood their reasons
We were aware of the responsibilities
Why didn't we remember the K?

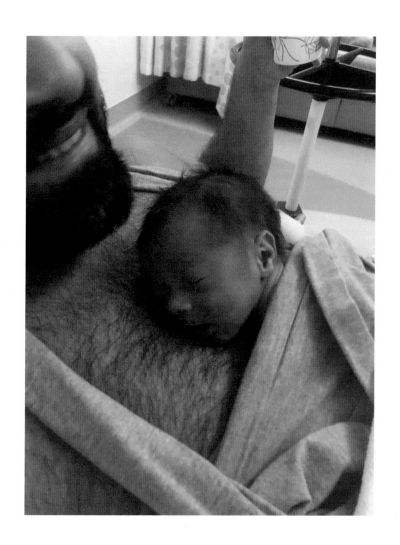

Dear Child
You're smiling at me
My heart is flowing
I can't explain
It's still a surreal feeling
I feel like I'm in a dream

K
I
R
A
N
KNEW
K
I
R
A
N
IS
KIND
K
I
R
A
N
IS
A
RAY
OF
LIGHT
KINDRED
KIND
K
I
R
A
N
I
S

KINDNESS

M

A

L

E

K

IS

KING

M

A

L

E

K

ENDS

WITH

A

"K"

Kangaroo Care

I
HAD
N
O
IDEA
SKIN
T
O
SKIN
OXY
T
O
C
I
N
MALEK
Y
O
U
ARE
S
L
E
E
P
I
N
G
ON
ME

YOU
A
R
E
GROWING
M
A
L
E
K
YOU
A
R
E
DEVELOP
I
N
G
I AM
H
O
L
D
I N G
O
N
TO
Y
O
U

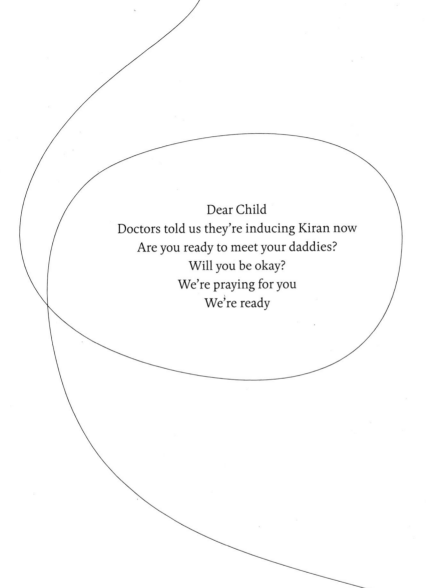

Dear Child
Doctors told us they're inducing Kiran now
Are you ready to meet your daddies?
Will you be okay?
We're praying for you
We're ready

Induction

You and I sit across from each other
The news hit hard
Barcelos's juicy chicken
Stares at us
No appetite
Overwhelming feelings
The fizz of the soda
Heightened sugar levels
"They're going to induce me."
A month and some days sooner
Anxiety and blood vessels
In waves
"Are you guys ready?"

34 Weeks and 2 Days

It's been two days
You and I trying to rest
on the waiting-room bed

It's been two hours
Oxytocin flowing within her blood
"Get out!"

We understood her emotions
We kept our distance
Few hours passed
Her silence
and light screams
"She's in active labour now."

At 4:00 a.m., it was the loudest scream

We walked into the room
Cervix dilated
Slowly, Malek's head

He arrived at 4:09 a.m.
A surreal feeling

Half-awake-half-asleep
Seemingly lifeless flesh
Surrounded by nurses
Together, as the intended parents,
We cut the umbilical cord
The flesh had a soul

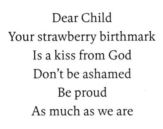

Dear Child
Your strawberry birthmark
Is a kiss from God
Don't be ashamed
Be proud
As much as we are

If I Hadn't Met You

Tarn, my Tarnooshi,
Among the hundreds of nicknames I have for you
If I hadn't met you, what would've happened?
Before meeting you, I was on the verge
I was going to marry a woman
start a family with her
Live a double life, secret unspoken lies
You would've lived in Philadelphia
Become a lawyer
We wouldn't have met
You would've ended up
with whoever
And I would've lived
another lie, another life
If I hadn't met you
I would've been lost

Cipralex—Part I

My family doctor discouraged me
"Antidepressants can be addictive."

I wasn't born this way
Depression became me
In the image of my father
I hadn't seen him in years
I missed him

"I need to feel good, doctor."
He prescribed me Cipralex

I wanted the magic pill, a quick fix
my father's face, his hands
I went down the dark

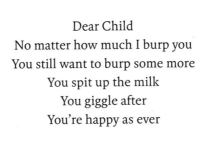

Dear Child
No matter how much I burp you
You still want to burp some more
You spit up the milk
You giggle after
You're happy as ever

Cipralex—Part II

I don't feel anything
I can walk, I can breathe
I can talk, I can smell
I'm still the same
Unhappy thoughts
I can't see my baba
I try another type
Popping pills
Pulsating panic
Jittery miserable

Cipralex—Part III

I forgot all their names
I've taken a few of them
They were all the same to me
Crushed powder
Insomniac nights
Suffocating
consuming
overwhelming
Love is not unconditional
When you are disowned
I question everything

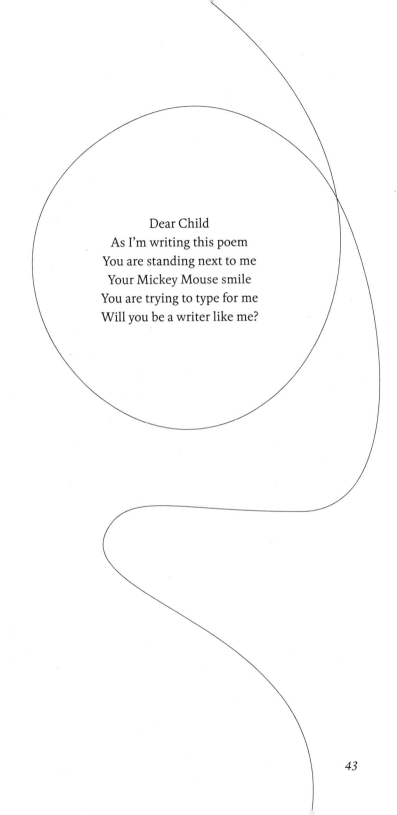

Dear Child
As I'm writing this poem
You are standing next to me
Your Mickey Mouse smile
You are trying to type for me
Will you be a writer like me?

Tired

The clock ticks and I lose every purpose
Every thought of my existence gone
Pills in
A lifeless soul feeling already dead
I felt worse than yesterday
Pills in
My feelings were deteriorating
Happiness was a fairy tale
Pills in
I no longer wanted to live
A life I could never pretend to live
Pills in

Is This the End?

My breaths were outnumbered
The pillow seemingly suffocating me
In the darkness, a white faint light
Tarn saved me
Held me tight, floating tears
"No more pills. No more."
Two weeks of a roller coaster
Crying just because
Unsure why
I have reached the top of the rabbit hole
I saw the light again

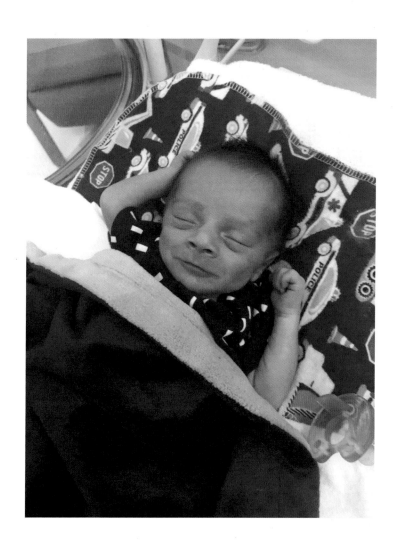

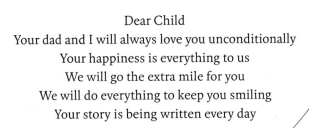

Dear Child
Your dad and I will always love you unconditionally
Your happiness is everything to us
We will go the extra mile for you
We will do everything to keep you smiling
Your story is being written every day

Your Love Saved Me

Dear Tarn, I'm writing this letter to you
As tears flow from my eyes.
They are tears of gratitude.
Thank you for saving me.
I was under the impression that I needed pills
I thought I was unhappy and depressed.
It was all situational temporary escape.
I had to dig deep into the roots
In order to find happiness from within.
Yes, it's not easy not having my father in my life.
But your love saved me.
I cannot express how much I love you.
Thank you for giving me strength
When I needed it the most.
Thank you for reminding me
That the flower has thorns too.
The flower can blossom.
The flower has life.

Industrial Scissors

It took years to heal
I tried to walk down the forest
Full of prickles, impossible
to move forward
The choice was in my hands
I had to pave the way.
I glanced behind and saw Tarn
Industrial scissors in hand
Together we cut through the prickles
Our way became clear
I threw the pills in the garbage
I never looked back
I found myself

Dear Child
After I married your dad
Some people didn't believe in our family
We faced a lot of hate
We kept each other strong
You are keeping us stronger

Our Silver and Blue Wedding

July 9, 2016:
We spent years in preparation
My whole body was numb
A part of me wanted my parents there
I wanted my father to walk me down the aisle
I knew it was impossible, but a man can dream sometimes
Instead, holding Tarn's hands as we walked inside
It gave me hope, it made me whole
The orchestral strings, a cinematic entrance
Surrounded by friends and family
I felt like I was in a dream, dressed like Cinderella
About to marry Prince Charming
We exchanged vows, in tears
When I looked through Tarn's eyes
I saw us holding a child again

Daycare

Time is the fleeting space between us
Months passed like seconds
Feeling separated, tears dwelling
I write this poem as a parent
Anxieties overflowing me
I miss you when you're learning
I'm writing this poem
When time is perpetual
Our emotions are cyclical
I wrote this poem outside
My heart a see-saw of emotions
Until I saw your smile outside

Dear Child
Our love is a fairy tale
You are a miracle story
God wanted you with us
We thank God every day
Our journey in a poem

Wedding Clip

A day after our magical wedding,
A clip mysteriously surfaced online
You and I were cutting the cake
You cut a piece and fed me
It went viral on Facebook
You told me not to read the comments
People were hating on us for being together
People shamed us, praying we would go to Hell
There was the odd supporter here and there
They didn't even let us enjoy ourselves
We were saddened but stayed strong
For the sake of our love

Death Threat

My Instagram was public before too
I'm not afraid to show the world our story
Photos of our stag party, us wearing tutus
Someone commented in Arabic
That they were embarrassed for me
That same account sent me a private message
Indicating that they know me, they know my name
They provided my full Arabic name
Hasan Namir Hasan Abood Il Ibrahim Al-Juboory
They threatened that they know where I live
They said that if I don't leave this boy, they will find me
They will hunt me down and wash away my sins with my blood
They used a fake account—they were afraid to face me
A coward threatening me to leave my soulmate
I'm not afraid to write about it

Dear Child
Your dad and I fought hard against hatred with love
We don't have any regrets
To think that I could've been killed once
God had another plan for all of us
Now I cherish my life with you

The Comedown

OUR
W
E
D
D
I
N
G
WAS
TEMPORARY
E
U
P
H
O
R
I
A
UNTIL
THREATS
F
E
A
R
W
O
R
R
Y
COWARDLY

W
H
Y
AM
I
NOT
H
A
P
P
Y
ANYMORE
THE
O
N
L
Y
THING
T
H
A
T
I
S
KEEPING
M
E
SANE
IS
Y
O
U

Formula Milk

Some babies are breastfed like I was
Others are formula-milk-fed like Tarn
Some say that breast milk is better for babies
Sometimes that's not an option
Our baby is formula-milk-fed
Positioning Malek upright
Supporting his neck and back with one hand
The other hand holding the bottle
Malek's lips latch on the bottle's nipple
He starts to drink
He stops as I angle the bottle
He needs breaks in between his feeds
I have him stay upright as I burp him
Gently rubbing his back
First attempt, second attempt
Then a loud burp
We're both happy

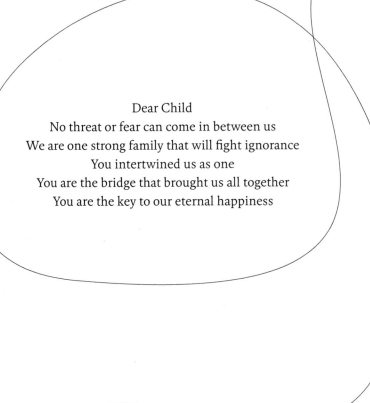

Dear Child
No threat or fear can come in between us
We are one strong family that will fight ignorance
You intertwined us as one
You are the bridge that brought us all together
You are the key to our eternal happiness

Fears and doubts trigger us
Our inner voices
Questioning our baby's health
Three pounds and a half
"Will he be okay?"
We asked that question endless times
"Are you afraid?"
"I just want him to be okay."
The umbilical cord was sentimental
Attached our hearts to Malek
I felt like he was living inside me
Since the day Kiran was pregnant
I didn't have to carry him or give birth
To have those feelings
"It's normal to worry."
"Should I be worrying all the time?"
"He's going to be fine."

Neonatal Intensive Care—Day II

Every night before I could even shut my eyes
I recited Qur'anic verses that always began like this:
In the Name of Allah, the Most Compassionate
the Most Merciful
My mother hadn't stopped praying
Your mother would pray every night, too
"Why are you afraid?"
"It's our son."
"God is great."
The nurses were like teachers
They taught us everything
"It's a blessing in disguise."
"Thank God always."

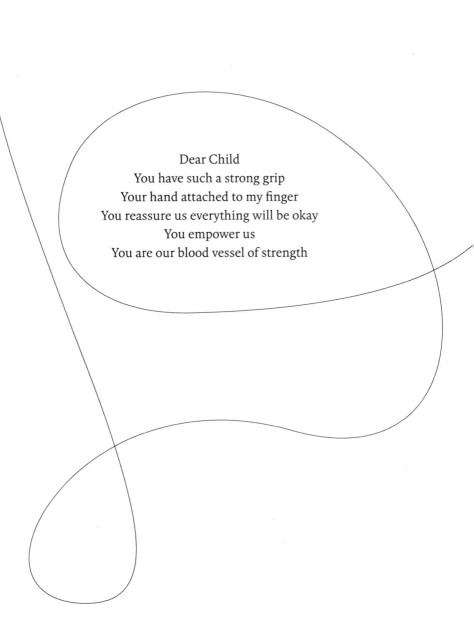

Dear Child
You have such a strong grip
Your hand attached to my finger
You reassure us everything will be okay
You empower us
You are our blood vessel of strength

Neonatal Intensive Care—Day III

Four and a half pounds of a soulful body
Holding on to me, counting on me to protect them
It's the greatest feeling
Sometimes I struggle to find the right words
In describing those feelings
My brain won't formulate them
I'm in awe as my dream is fulfilled
Nurses roam around all the time
Heart monitor starts beeping
I freak out as the nurse reassures me
"False alarm."
For the next two weeks, I live, breathe
in beeps
One beat at a time

Neonatal Intensive Care—Discharge Day

November 9, 2019

Nine is the number that saved me
The nurse was happy for us
We get to take our Malek home
"Are you excited or nervous?"
I'm grateful

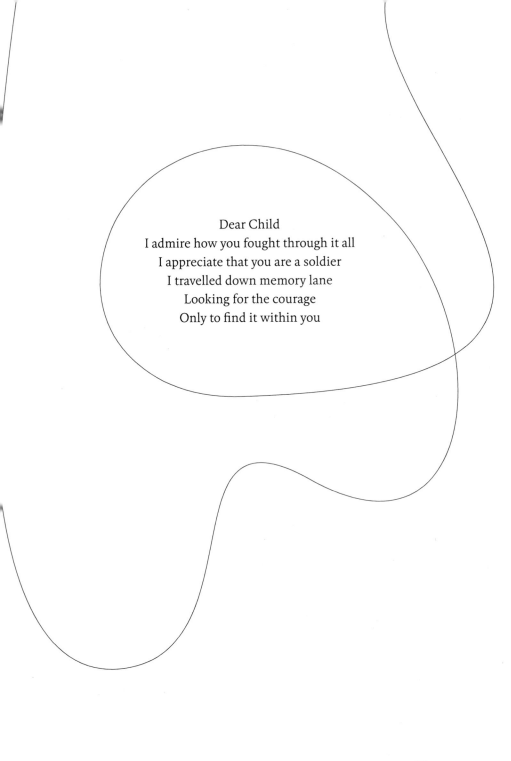

Dear Child
I admire how you fought through it all
I appreciate that you are a soldier
I travelled down memory lane
Looking for the courage
Only to find it within you

Car Seat

There is always something that's nerve-wracking
Making sure your baby is secured
There are all these rules and parent groups
You can post a photo of your baby in the car seat
You can ask for a car-seat check
This is my biggest challenge and fear
My child's safety is everything

Netflix and Parenting

When it was just You and I
It was Netflix and Chill
Our lips sliding over our tongues
Our bodies like clay ceramics
Morphing into one
A surrogate who wiped the question mark
Malek in his bassinet sleeping
We turn on Netflix in between
Binge-watch every show
This is the new life
As the credits roll in black
"What should we watch next?"

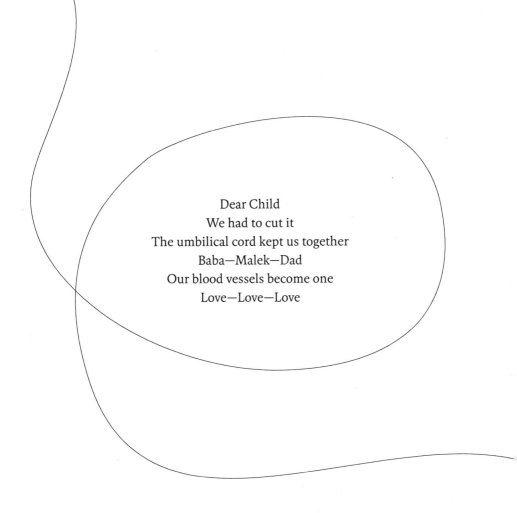

Dear Child
We had to cut it
The umbilical cord kept us together
Baba—Malek—Dad
Our blood vessels become one
Love—Love—Love

Cry Interrupted

As the queen sheds a tear on *The Crown*
The third season
I hear another cry in our room
coming from baby's bassinet.
We pause our show and walk inside
I carry Malek in my arms.
"We just fed him, didn't we?"
"Yeah. Why is he crying?"
His diaper has been changed already.
He has been burped already.
"Burp him some more."
I burped him and held him.
He stopped crying.
"That's love."

Emails and Photos

Yes, I'm that kind of parent.
Who has created an email account for Malek
I have shared this idea with Tarn:
"Habibi,
Let's make an email account for Malek.
Let's send him photos and stuff
throughout his childhood."
"Wow, that's a great idea."
"When he turns sixteen, we will share the account with him."
When he turns sixteen, Inshallah-Waheguru,
He will see everything unfold until that age.
His childhood and baby adventures
All the special moments and photos.
I want to see the diamond magic in his eyes.
I can't wait to see his face.
Yes, I'm that kind of parent.

Dear Child
You looked me in the eye and smiled
I teared up—it's still so surreal
This poem is a dream
You helped me write it
The most beautiful dream

Gender Reveal

I wrote most of these poems here
While you were on my chest in a kangaroo-style outfit
These poems are not written in chronological order
I look back and recall your gender reveal party, Malek
Your auntie Alexandra prepared something wonderful
The surprises were the pink and blue eggs that we crushed
But none of these eggs were runny
We went outside, everyone holding a confetti cannon
We all went at once, my heart was racing
We were showered in blue to my excitement
I knew that you were our Malek from day one
My heart kept saying Malek not Maleka
Though we would've loved you the exact same
Always unconditionally

Lullabies

My baby
My sweet Malek
Let me wipe your tears
Let me hold you
Everything will be okay
So long as you're in my arms
You will grow and thrive
You will shine like a star

Our baby
Our king Malek
Our king Malek
You give us hope, our love
Let us hold you
Everything is bright
So long as you're in our arms
You are every bit of us
You are our dream come true

Our prince and king
Our sun and moon
Our night and day
Our east and west
Our heart and soul
Our apple and orange
Our baby and child
Our habibi and hayati

1...2...3...4
Here we go
    Cheer up
    Be happy
        Smile
        Don't cry
            5...6...7...8
            Don't frown
            Upside down
                Smile
                9...10...
                    Smile
                    Our angel

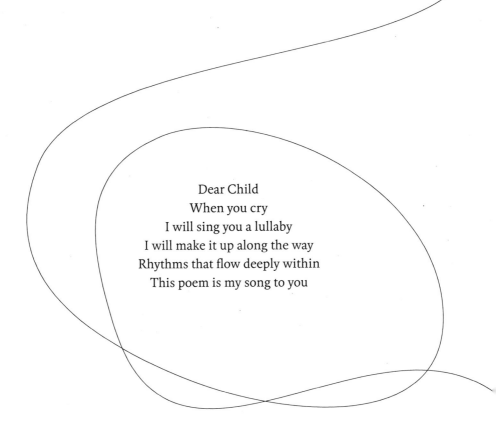

Dear Child
When you cry
I will sing you a lullaby
I will make it up along the way
Rhythms that flow deeply within
This poem is my song to you

Christmas Parental Duties

- Put Up Christmas Tree
- Caffeinate Tarn
- Put Up Christmas Ornaments
- Heat Up Leftover Food
- Be Excited a Month Early
- Wipe the Whole House Down
- Decorate for Christmas Spirit
- Kiss Tarn Every Morning
- Watch Malek Smile
- Wear Christmas Clothes
- Feed Malek Milk and Hum
- Make Christmas More Joyful

Watermarks

Your face turns red, pearl droplets washing over
You have been fed, you have been burped
Your diaper has been changed, you are cozy
Let me hold you, let me tell you everything will be all right
Let me try tapping on your back gently, all right, let's try this...
You are bundled up, I hold you on my chest
Two fleeting minutes and you are deep asleep
Our touch is more magical than water

Dear Child
Our blood is a river of thick water
Transported from our hearts into yours
The umbilical cord a metaphysical mode
Water keeps us all alive
While our blood is our love confirmed

"Your Baby Will Be Confused"

Men and women can reproduce
God created the female to bring children
so they say, but love is not a function

"The baby won't be able to say mama."
But he is going to have a dad and baba
We understand science, biology, and religion
We know that men and women make babies
"But what will you tell your son?"

We will tell him to love whoever he wants
We will support him if he likes women
We will not raise our son to be gay
We will raise our son to be human
"Stop confusing your son."
"Your brain needs rewiring."

We will not raise our child in a fairy tale
We will be realistic
We will not hide the truth
We will not deny science, biology, and religion
I didn't fall in love with a woman, I fell in love with a man
My family isn't like the other families, but whose family is?

Normal

Sometimes, the thoughts cross my mind
There will be backlash
There will be bullying
Some people will not understand
"Who cares what people think?"
I want Malek to be proud of us
Peers and parents
I can hear their voices: "No!"
I can see their judgmental eyes
their sideways glances
"This is not normal."

Dear Child
We will always be transparent
Don't ever fear we will never hide the truth
You are our child our king our pride
We are your daddies
Baba + Dad + Malek = family

The Truth Is...

Let's step back for a minute
Let us reflect and be happy
Our love broke through
The impossibilities
"I'm proud of us."

"The truth is I'm not afraid."
I lived my whole life worrying about rejection
Trying to be accepted by others
"What would people think?"
"Mama, what about people?"

The truth is, people will talk
People will stare and say, "That's enough."
Let them be, "I don't blame them."
Let us be, "We're not wanting."
"This is our family."

The truth is waiting
Already seen in their eyes
"Look at them."

Your Smile, My Kangaroo

You don't like sleeping in your bassinet
You want to be in my arms, or your dad's
The hospital gave us the kangaroo outfit
A clothing pouch with straps
Tied to protect and keep you within
The design promotes skin-to-skin
Within me, all the oxytocin feels
"The more, the better."
I am like the kangaroo holding his child
You are trying to fight your sleep
You want to be present in the moment
Your smile gives me life even when I'm low
I pray to God to protect you, my kangaroo

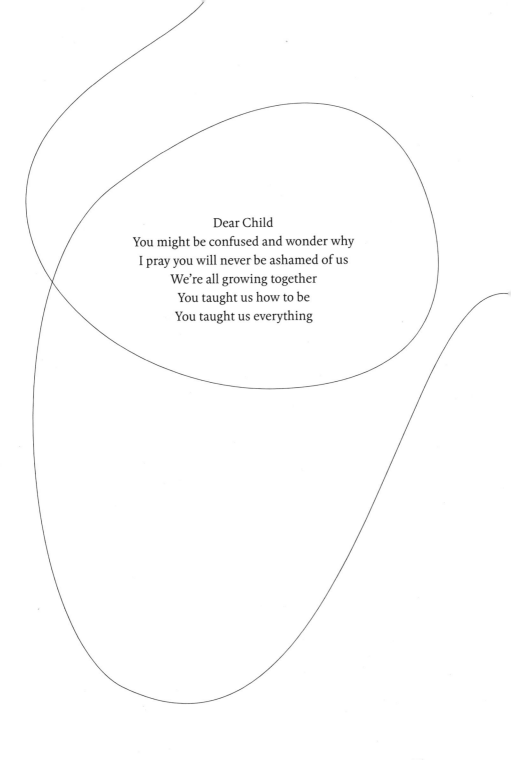

Dear Child
You might be confused and wonder why
I pray you will never be ashamed of us
We're all growing together
You taught us how to be
You taught us everything

Tummy Time

We learned each day
to lay you on your stomach
A minute more added daily
Lying down on the floor, crying
Uncomfortably new
A reflex in the works
You are exploring new territories
There is discomfort and pain, those tears
A minute added each day, less crying
"Don't be afraid, you're a fighter."
These were the longest minutes for both of us
"I know this is for the best, habibi."
Don't cry my angel, it's tummy time

Pregnancy Symptoms

When Kiran was feeling sick
I was feeling sick, too
Nausea that wasn't symbolic
Pebbles of bile rising up
The feeling was real
My child inside
waiting for us
I spoke to him
every morning
and night, hoping
he would hear me
He would recognize
my voice. That feeling
like a hair stuck in my throat
The urge to gag
my stomach was empty
I could feel you with me, my son

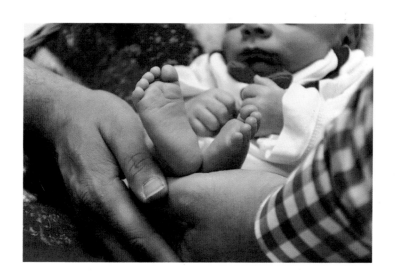

Dear Child
Take your time fight through it all
We are with you every step of the way
You are sitting up on your own
You are trying to walk
You do you on your own pace

They Told Her

They Told Her:

"You can't take a hot bath, Kiran."

"Doctor said no intercourse until heartbeat."

"No pop."

"Eat more."

"You're eating for two."

"You have high blood pressure."

"You have gestational diabetes."

"You have pre-eclampsia."

"You don't need to stress out."

"They're inducing you early."

Delivery

We stood near the door, watching life happen in front of our eyes

It was our first time experiencing birth together

My mind swimming with thoughts and questions

Kiran's pain and joy, a roller-coaster ride of feelings on my face

We were at the top just before the drop

My heart almost stopped when she pushed, screaming

Out came Malek and my heart beat again

Dear Child
I could scream and let the whole world know
You are our euphoria
We want you to be happy always
As long as you're feeling it too
We are on cloud nine with you

Ray of Light

Forgiveness, the Ray of Light

You have given us the greatest gift

You have been so kind to us

"I'm sorry."

We've all made mistakes

We're all human beings

"I'm sorry again."

Don't be sorry

It wasn't easy

"I wish I could go back."

We can't reverse time

We can only move forward

"Do you forgive me?"

Yes, my dear

Everything can heal

Fear of Attachment

Our feelings of appreciation
Are the acknowledgment of human feelings.

Kiran, my sister-in-law and our surrogate
You carried our child for many months.

You worried about getting too close.
Your feelings were valid and entitled.

"I can't help with the attachment."
We never feared or mistrusted you.

We understood and stood by you.
"No, we are not worried," we said.

You will forever be his aunt.
We are forever grateful for you.

Dear Child
Before you can ask, we will tell you the truth
Kiran is your aunt, we are your parents
Families come in different sizes and forms
You are our child and forever will be
That's what matters the most

Photo Shoot

Your Christmas hat fit your head perfectly
Your aunt, my amazing co-worker, knitted it for you
This was the first time we were taking you out
since neonatal intensive care
The air was chilly, the ground covered in snow
You were enamoured by the bright lights
You looked so cute in that car seat
You were probably wondering where we were
Tina was our photographer
Talented and patient
Matching Christmas sweaters
Family photos
Fotos
You kept smiling like you knew what was happening
You were a natural

The Nest

My bird, your wings were never broken
They are just growing and glowing
I want you to fly far to places
we cannot yet imagine

My bird, your voice shines through
Your small throat cooing, encouraging
I want you to achieve what's not achieved

My bird, your story is written before you
Be proud of your roots and teach others
So that we may all live in one united world

Dear Child
This poem roots back
The family tree grows with you
We are rooted in you
You take us back through time
The memories make us smile

Nesting

"I just want everything clean."
"Do I have to explain my sudden energy?"
"Have you heard of nesting?"
"What's that?"
I'll explain it to you
You forget about it for a little bit
"Just getting ready for baby."
Don't question my energy
I'll do what I want
"My moods swing."
Yeah, you'll just have to believe me
"We believed you."
We did everything
"No, no, trust me, I was nesting."
I was being near to birth

Lawyer Contract

$5,000

Documents

Assistant

Signatures

Mind change

Embryo transfer

Fertility Clinic

Nine months

Requirement

Mood swings

Intended parents

Changing mind

Signed

Surrogate

Dear Child
I lost count how many times I kissed your head
You are babbling words
Dad + Baba
I said I love you
You said I love you

50/50

You let me sleep in during the day
When I let you sleep during the night
See-Saw
Equal parenting
Switching shifts
You and I alternate universes
Taking turns to live in the moment
See-Saw
Ample opportunities
Alternate schedules
You and I, equal forces

Alexa

My child sleeps in his crib
The room a hundred feet away from me
Years ago, they used walkie-talkies
"Amazon Alexa is amazing, eh?"
I drop in wirelessly to hear Malek
the soothing purr from his bassinet

Dear Child
When I looked through your eyes
I saw myself in my father's arms
Your grandfather saw me in you
You are the bridge that connects us
I hope I can see him someday too

Crying Interpretations

Some cries are hunger
Some cries are poop discomfort
Some cries are purple
Some cries are red
Some cries are lonely
Some cries are loud
Some cries are whines
Some cries are gassy
Some cries are laughs
Some cries are pain
Some cries are constipation
Some cries are needy
Some cries are urine
Some cries are thirst
Some cries are fatigue
Some cries are cold
Some cries are warm
Some cries are confusing
Some cries make sense
Some cries are clean
Some cries are dirty
Some cries are real
Some cries are fake

Christmas 2019

"This is absolutely the best.
Especially in today's world.
No shame in love
Merry Christmas."

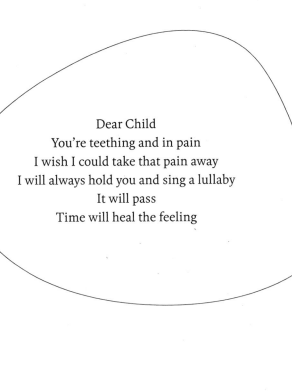

Dear Child
You're teething and in pain
I wish I could take that pain away
I will always hold you and sing a lullaby
It will pass
Time will heal the feeling

Some Sleepless Nights

Right now, I'm an insomniac and can't help it
Malek and Tarn are both sleeping
I tried to shut my eyes, my heart racing
"Please, don't send me photos like that."
Photos of two men and a baby
Ten years, still clinging to the same dream
The dream of seeing your son with a woman and kids
My eyelid stuttering in the same wavelength
Tarn's snoring a stable rhythm
I'm just going to wait for Malek's next feed
2:20 a.m.—approximately forty more minutes
"I dreamed of your family being different."
Yours was the same dream as mine
I dreamed we cross the bridge together
Grandparents, aunts, parents, and Malek
"Don't blame me for being sleepless."

Eye See

Went to the mall with Malek
Eyes see you left, right, centre, north and south
"It's new to them. They're not used to us."
Their eyes don't necessarily judge us
"They're curious or confused."
Or they love how fab we are as parents
Either way, let them look, it's inevitable
"As long as they don't attack us."
"I see."

Dear Child
We dreamed of your birthday
A big celebration in a hall
Surrounded by our family and loved ones
We were in a pandemic
The air around us changed all that

They See

"Look at them."

"Shame on them."

"Where is the mom?"

"A candy cane to the mom, too."

"How?"

"I don't get it—how?"

"Wow."

"Wow."

"Wow."

Malek (Written by Tarn Khare)

Daddy and Baba
Change looms near
The hum of his tiny voice
The beginning of a new chapter
A little bit of both of us
Diaper to be changed
Baba and Daddy

Dear Child
We still celebrated your birthday
A huddle of us and yet
It was small
It was intimate
Everything was perfect

Feeding

Feeding you, Malooky, as you hold my finger with your hand, is the greatest feeling I feel every day! In one hand, I'm holding a blue bowl of wheat biscuit cereal, mixed with formula milk. In my other hand, I'm holding a matching blue spoon. You are sitting in your high chair, your smile elevates mine. I take a scoop of the oatmeal and feed it to you. Your eyes light up like diamonds as you chew the food. I cannot explain that feeling because it's greater than what I could put into words.

Ever since Daddy Tarnooshi went back to work, Malooky you've been my best friend and my sunshine, even though we miss Daddy very much! I thank God every day that I get to take care of you and hold you in my arms forever Inshallah-Waheguru! I love you and your daddy more than anything! May God protect you and bless you always our angel, xo

Love,

Baba Hasan

Hide-and-Seek

Sometimes when I was young, I used to play hide-and-seek
It was dark, I felt safe as Mama watched over me from a distance
Even when I had nightmares, I woke up feeling safe in Mama's
    arms
When Baba played dominoes with his friends, when Baba was
    over there
Mama was the one running around taking care of us three
When I turned right or left, when I was scared, Mama was there

When I was a baby, I used to play with my mom's curls
When Malek was a baby, he played with my facial hair

Sometimes when I was young, I used to hide from a lot of things
Ready or not, here I come

I was lost in the darkness. I couldn't breathe anymore
When I looked up, I saw my mama's face and I felt safe

When I was a baby, my mama used to feed me a tomato-and-rice
    soup
When Malek was a baby, my mama fed her grandson the same
    soup

Dear Child
You are a hopeful message
You are the messenger of love
The year blinks in an eye
I'm still in this dream.
Am I allowed to pause?

I Am a Father

I remember one time you were carrying me on your shoulders
I was two years old, I could still feel safe in my memory
You would take me to the store to buy some candy
You gave me everything I wanted, you bought me everything
I needed
You were the best friend who loved me, but couldn't accept
everything
I was young when you told me you would pay for my wedding
In fact I insisted that I would pay for my own wedding
I was once into acting and wanted to win an Oscar
You told me that you dreamed that I would be a famous author
We shared a mutual dream but when I fulfilled it,
you weren't there
Instead you stood with them, ashamed of me, when you knew
all along
I'm not going to say that I'm going to be a better father than you
Now that God has gifted me with your grandson Malek
Because you were a great father and I'm so thankful to be
your son
You saw me in your grandson, and I will always speak well
of you
I will always teach my son that you were a great father
I can't remember the last time I was in your arms
Don't worry, I still pray that we meet once again
Even for just one minute, a quick wave for all the years
Twenty-some years of a father-&-son bond
I promise you that I will always be my son's baba
I will support him in any path he wants to take
I don't blame you for standing with them
I am a father and you are mine

I Am a Mother

When I was young I wanted to be a girl
I liked playing with Barbie dolls
I love belly dancing
I love imitating divas
I had baby Barbies
I knew I wanted to be a mother
Yet I'm a man, with motherly feelings
I moved on with those feelings
I had to be a man and marry a woman
I could only be a father, not a mother
I didn't have breasts, I had empty nipples
I realized I didn't have to wear a dress to be a mother
It's not an appearance, it's a feeling
I've always been the one worrying about everyone
I could be a man who loves another man
When Daddy is at work
I am drawn to you the way
the umbilical cord is a feeling
I am a mother

Dear Child
Your parents switch roles
We are your mother and father
Our family is unique like us
God brought us all together
The umbilical cord is forever

Umbilical Cord

This is the thread of life
A lifetime commitment
My ancestors and genes in milky white
Your dad's legacy in an egg
XY YX XY YX XY YX XY YX XY YX
"Please attach." Sleepless nights
Interfaith prayers from Mama and Mum
Surrogate couldn't wait to tell us the news
She secretly took the pregnancy test
I
W
A
S
SPEECHLESS
I felt the umbilical cord grafting to my flesh
I felt your heartbeat long before the ultrasound
Tender particles of roses folded on our heads
The gender-reveal ceremony made me wonder
My heart knew I wanted you Malek, but you could've been
Maleka
There were fears and doubts intervening aggressively
We were thankful for you, regardless of your sex; the confetti
was blue
The umbilical cord that kept us floating on the king's throne
You were ready for us, as long as we were ready for you
Inside the womb, you were growing, becoming both of us
The umbilical cord is thousands of years of intersectionality
Rooting in the Euphrates and Singapore Rivers
As the water waves through the Pacific Ocean
Your dad and I stood on the bridge, waiting for you
I met him on April 9, 2011, when I saw you waiting for us
"You didn't want to wait anymore."

32
W
E
E
K
S
4
D
A
Y
S
6 WEEKS
EARLY
You just wanted to be with your dad and baba
This was your umbilical cord
Baba and Dad cut through it
The string which life flowed through
Blood vessels pumped through your heart
Your cry was so soft, yet loud enough to announce arrival
You have my eyes and your dad's ears and nose
You have my forehead and your dad's light hair
You are us and we are you in every single way possible
Dear child, this book is a letter of hope
Like the umbilical cord that kept us dreaming
Someday, the three of us will stand together on the bridge
We will watch our rivers converge with the ocean

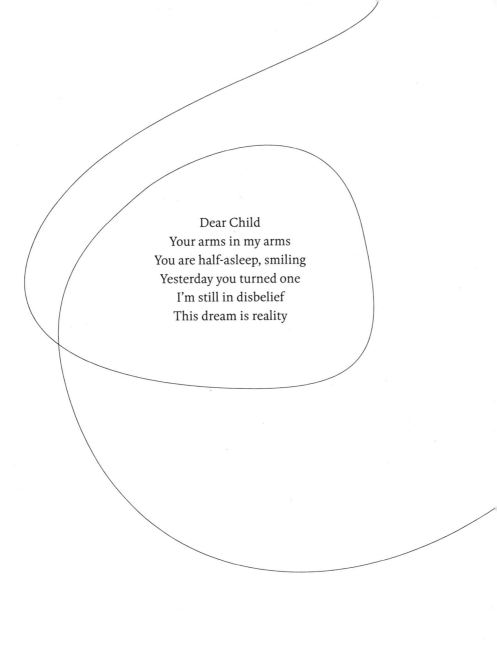

Dear Child
Your arms in my arms
You are half-asleep, smiling
Yesterday you turned one
I'm still in disbelief
This dream is reality

Photo Credits

Photo #7
"Our Hands and Malek's Feet" by Tina Clelland

Photo # 8
"Malek's Christmas Photo" by Tina Clelland

Photo # 9
"Malek in My Arms" by John Bello

Photo # 10
"Love is a Painting" by John Bello, painting by Cathryn John

Acknowledgements

I want to thank God for everything in my life, most specially for gifting me and Tarn with Malek. I want to endlessly thank my angelic sister-in-law Kiran for helping us bring Malek into this world. Thank you to my wonderful parents, sisters, family from both sides, and my friends for their continued love and support throughout our journeys. I love you all very much.

I want to thank my amazing and incredible publishers Jay MillAr and Hazel Millar (Book*hug Press) for continuously believing in my work. You fulfilled my poet's dream by publishing my first poetry book, *War/Torn*. Working with you both is a continuous joy and an experience I will always cherish.

Thank you so much to my brilliant editor and friend Shazia Hafiz Ramji. We worked together for the first time on my poetry book *War/Torn* and to my luck, we got to work together again on *Umbilical Cord*. You make the editing process so wonderful and you've made such a positive impact on my poetry.

I want to thank Gareth Lind of Lind Design for the vivid and colourful cover that wowed me from the first sample drafts. Thank you kindly to Shannon Whibbs for your precise and excellent copy edits of the book.

As a poet and an author, I'm inspired by so many other poets and authors whose works capture my heart and soul. Thank you so much to those who have helped pave the way for me and for your endless support in my career.

I wrote *Umbilical Cord* as a love letter to my heart and soul, Tarn and Malek, whom I both love endlessly. It is dedicated to all types of families as a message of support and love and hope.

About the Author

Hasan Namir is an Iraqi-Canadian author. He graduated from Simon Fraser University with a BA in English and received the Ying Chen Creative Writing Student Award. He is the author of *God in Pink* (2015), which won the Lambda Literary Award for Best Gay Fiction and was chosen as one of the Top 100 Books of 2015 by *The Globe and Mail*. His work has also been in media across Canada. He is also the author of poetry book *War/Torn* (2019, Book*hug Press), which received the 2020 Barbara Gittings Honor Book Award from the Stonewall Book Awards, and children's book *The Name I Call Myself* (2020). Hasan lives in Vancouver with his husband and child.

Colophon

Manufactured as the first edition of
Umbilical Cord
in the fall of 2021 by Book*hug Press

Edited for the press by Shazia Hafiz Ramji
Copy edited by Shannon Whibbs
Text + design by Gareth Lind
Type: Kievit Serif and Nitti

bookhugpress.ca